A.P. BASTIAN

A DIRTY WORD CALLED GRIEF

Print ISBN: 978-1-09833-422-2 | eBook ISBN: 978-1-09833-423-9

For Paul James Scheffler and all those on their journey to befriend grief.

People have grown uncomfortable with tears so they bypass sadness by gifting you words they think will help you to hear: *Everything happens for a reason*, they say, and you nod politely when you want to scream because not only are they afraid to feel your loss with you, their expression is leftovers of what someone once served them and they never stopped to determine if they are still good to ingest or need to be tossed out. They don't even know what they're saying anymore. The words just come out now, as an automatic pre-programmed response to grief.

And all you want is for them to hold you in silence, for them to tell you the truth about death and not shy away from experiencing darkness with you. All you want is to be accepted as the shell of a human loss has made of you, to be seen, even with grief weighing down every bone of your body. Hell, especially because of it.

It is true that no one can make you feel better about your loss, but you should know that you're not alone, that it is possible to feel so much heartache and yet still feel numb, that it's ok if you can't get out of bed for a few days, or if you can't help but stay busy in an attempt to keep yourself safe from the sadness, albeit temporarily.

Solitude always comes.

The overwhelming waves of grief will find you, no matter what.

In those moments, when the waves come crashing down and the only sounds you can make are sobs and screams and your body curls itself into a ball and you're so angry and so sad and afraid, all at once-

Those moments are what these words are for.

I know your pain.

You're not alone.

Let yourself grieve.

Give yourself love.

CONTENTS

PROLOGUE

He laid covered by a white sheet, wearing his favorite plaid shirt that I helped his mother pick, eyes closed, lips purple and hands carefully overlapping each other on top of his hard chest. His eyelashes were as long as ever, his fingernails blue, cold.

So cold.

I touched him so my brain would register what my eyes already knew: he wasn't there. He wasn't sleeping. And even if he was, this is a dream I would never see him wake up from.

Not this time.

So I kissed his lips. I buried my head on his chest. I spilled my tears on his shirt as I told him I loved him, one last time; as I thanked him for everything, one last time.

And now I cry. Still. On public transportation, during breaks at work, on top of my lovers and pillows, over my phone and cards he wrote me in perfect calligraphy. I cry and I scream at how unfair life seems. The good die young and the young die good and I'm still alive and not well and there's nothing good about the way he went.

The clocking in and out doesn't feel real. The mealtimes and pastimes and friends' laughter feels like a fog, just a part of all the non-quintessential things that make up my life these days.

I'm not dead.

But I'm not alive either.

All I know to tell them when they ask me if I'm fine is this:

I'm still breathing.

That's all I have.

That's all I know.

My breath is rising in and out of my chest.

GRIEF IS A
DIRTY WORD
I LIKE TO SAY
IN MOUTHFULS

No one speaks of grief.

The world seems to be
unprepared
for the aftermath
of death.

I wish someone would have warned me:

listen, you'll be shattered in places
you didn't even know
existed before.

but the dead can't speak and
the living are clueless
because they decided
that the worst of the dirty words
is the one called

grief.

I can't tell you how many days after it happened, but suddenly I felt the urge to know exactly what happens to our bodies when we die.

What happened to *his* body.

I found myself obsessed with the subject, researching the topic for hours online, staying up late reading on the vacuum that is the world wide web everything I could find.

Far from being dead, a rotting corpse is teeming with life.

Rotting.

I didn't even make a note or highlight. I knew the word would be immediately engraved in my mind. And once it was, others came to join it:

Decomposition.

Self-digestion.

Autolysis.

Putrefaction.

Discoloration of the body, I learned, was caused by anaerobic bacteria feeding on the body's tissues, and as a result, fermenting the sugars in them to produce gaseous by-products, which in turn lead to bloating.

His blue fingernails.

His purple lips.

These gases continue to build up causing blisters on the skin's surface, followed by loosening of the skin.

The gash on his head.

How did they manage to keep him looking like him if they found his body two days after he took his last breath?

I'm sure his entire face and hands were covered in makeup by the time I got to see him.

Cold on a metal table.

Gone.

In that moment there were no words to describe what I felt when I saw whatever parts were left of him held together by science.

No amount of research could have prepared me for that.

*How will I live when everything I see makes me
think about death?*

Chautauqua House

We all gathered to honor and remember him

silently

and that morning I recall

giving myself ten minutes to cry

before doing my makeup

and the unraveling of the perfect exterior that followed

the words I said out loud to comfort hearts

while mine shattered inside.

Afterwards we all said

that was nice, he would have liked that

but what did we know?

He wasn't around to share his ideas

on the aftermath of death.

We gave all his things away.

it was horrible.

seeing every piece of him handed off to strangers and
family members
merely because they happened to be the ones
still breathing.

I tell everyone I love them lately

I linger in my hugs and

let strangers feed me.

I have been kissing. a lot.

and I have never felt so broken and whole,

all at once, before.

It's a weird space I'm trying to embrace:

shattered.

I try

desperately

to hang on to every little part of him left

every fragment,

no matter how small.

I refuse to live as if because his body is gone

every other part of him has to be, too.

I see them mentally take two steps back, afraid of my emotions, of the weight of the word grief. They think they will be sucked in by the vortex of my sadness. What they don't understand is that this kind of broken isn't contagious. It isn't some virus that goes around, multiplying itself until we all have it.

it is **mine**.

only mine to share.

Let me feel proud of my fragile strength.
I'm not afraid to feel.
The only thing I fear is
being numb again.

Do you remember being born and the pain of leaving the warm
home of the womb
for the unknown? You cried so many tears that day.
And yet. Given the choice, wouldn't you do it again?

This grief is my rebirth.

Don't stunt my growth because you can't remember
how painful it is to lose the only home
you've ever known.

I have started to own this grief

I'm not going to hide it away like some shameful sin any longer.

I will bring it up on first dates, share it like

small bites of chocolates with my roommates on the couch,

drown in it as if it were a giant glass of red wine;

I will scream it out of me and into pillows and

bring the subject with me to dinners and various bars

across town, neatly tucked in my clutch

like my favorite lipstick.

I'm going to own this grief

and you're going to watch me

so that the next time they ask me how I'm handling things

I can look them in the eye and say

I'm handling it just fine, thanks.

Right now I smell of smoke
and if you were to lick my cheeks
you would taste salt water.

My lips are cherry-stained from red wine
and my body whole
though my bones feel heavy and cold.

Everything changed since he left.
and yet time drags on.

What day is it?

How long has it been?

I start counting time on my fingertips
as if math made a difference

as if time would give reason
to this grief.

I want to die,

I prayed to God

asked the Almighty

why didn't he take me instead?

I am angry that I'm still alive.

I am angry that everyone else is, too.

Everyone else but him.

I would trade myself and the rest of the world for him if I could.

When they ask me how I did it,

how I survived grief,

I will tell them it was by letting it take all of me-

piece by piece

bit by bit

until I grew comfortable with it being

just another indispensable

part of me.

Today I'll allow myself to give in

to the grief that has made itself at home in my heart.

the tired muscles and foggy brain,

the struggle of admitting that he is gone,

the immeasurable longing to hear him tell me

it will all be ok

one more time

one last time

feel his arms around me giving me the strength I never believed
I had

until the day he passed away

and proved it to me.

what a bastard.

he was always right about everything.

just a little less

maybe I should make friends with his demons-
you know, the ones he left here.

maybe I should name them
so it feels less weird.

Holidays

so it's time to celebrate

and no one says his name

except for me.

loudly and in mouthfuls.

it's not that they want to forget him.

they just don't want to remember his death.

They tell me how I should feel

It'll pass, they say

so every day before I set foot outside

I place an armor around me

I can do this, I say

knowing full well that part of me just wants to crawl back inside and die.

Don't say that! they seem upset.

but these are the feelings I hide behind this mask of strength.

Most days I can be who they want me to be.

just not today.

Please, for God's sake and his,

just give today to me and this grief.

If the dead could see the living

they would be afraid

of the ghosts

we carry.

My cry has changed since he died-

it's different now

silent

mundane even

Now the tears take over when they please

without the need for a reason or excuse.

Grief starts to feel

as natural as breathing

these first ninety days

without him.

Don't mistake

my vulnerability

for weakness

there is strength in my tears

and thorns in my love.

His mom and I decided

that we would trade our lives for his.

now tell me that isn't what love is.

Life is short.

Everybody knows it.

but it's so different-

when you start to feel it

in your bones.

Why do people talk about survival

as if it's the greatest thing on earth?

some days living broken is harder

than

      dying

          whole.

Have a great day! he says

as he flashes me his most earnest smile

I'm bare-faced, tear-stained

crying in public transportation again

but I say *thanks*

and step into the snow in mid-March.

Around the bend I make my way back to the music house

searching for things to kick as I walk

fantasizing about screaming so loud that I swallow the world, whole

and all that's left is a white screen-

serene.

Hard days, some days

have their way with me.

Southwark Cathedral

I lit a candle for him.
The chapel was empty and light was still shining through the
stained glass windows,
casting dancing shadows on the ornate tile floor.
I don't know why I did it, but I lit a candle for him
and as soon as I did,
I ran out clutching my heart and gasping for air
and I stood in the courtyard
holding back tears as I admired the exquisite gothic architecture
trying my hardest to avoid being sucked into the vortex of sadness,
to avoid drowning in another wave of grief.

Still. I lit that candle for him.
I don't even know why
he never believed in these things, and neither do I.

Maybe I lit that candle to keep him alive

somewhere between the archways of the cathedral and tombs of
the sacred that have come to pass.

But when I lit that candle I lost my breath
because the only thing I can do for him now
is light a fucking candle.
and that doesn't solve anything;
it doesn't mean anything;
it doesn't change anything;
it doesn't bring him back from the dead.

Still.
I lit that candle.
Maybe so others would know that I once loved and lost
deeply, too.
I once believed in something, too.

Maybe I lit that candle
for me.

We wanted to blame someone

or something,

at the very least

find a cause

but sometimes

there really is no one to blame

in both life

and death.

Are you alright?

they care so much

but know so little

of this grief I carry inside

I'm not alright, I say

but I don't tell them that I don't think I'll ever be-

I care too much and know enough

to see them break for me.

We met over coffee and talked about our last and upcoming trips. The first words out of his mouth when he saw me were *you look taller in your pictures*. I should have known then to leave. But I do that sometimes- let people say whatever they have to say to me.

The second time I saw him, he read my words out loud as he laid in bed beside me and said, his eyes still fixed on the computer screen: *close the door*. I guess my words served as an aphrodisiac to him then. I could tell by the way he touched my skin that life hadn't been fair to him either. It was as if his fingers bore the bruises on his heart.

And who am I to turn down a broken-hearted guy?

I closed my eyes as I let him take me

let him make both of us

forget.

I drown myself

in sex and alcohol
so I can remember

what it was like

to feel

alive.

Who are you? he asks,

What should I call you? he continues

and I'm still not listening because I don't care about what he has to say. Suddenly my red lips are on his right earlobe as I whisper, an octave lower than usual, pronouncing each word slowly, my tongue dancing in my mouth:

You can call me whatever you want.

My fingers, nails painted forest green and peeking from long, black gloves, reach for the buttons of his shirt and I no longer give a fuck about the rest of the world.

all I want is the weight of his body on mine, to give this whip a try

so I can forget this day

forget his death

and feel alive

(even if just for a little while).

That Girl

I had sex with his friend, but only after we shared our tears,

and another time I got too drunk and threw up as I cried and became intimate with the toilet in the bathroom of a closed down club in Aspen at a private party he would have adored.

I kept saying *this is all just so fucked up*, over and over until a friend hugged me with so much love I felt, albeit momentarily, as if it was all going to be alright.

Hugs can do that sometimes.

Since then I've donned leather and lace late at night as I strutted around looking for trouble, slowly undressing a handsome man I met on the street, and

I have fallen asleep holding her close and desiring lips in a way I never have before.

All this to say I don't know who I am these days.

I don't know who to be

without
him.

At times I feel like an idiot, sitting on the couch, hands on my head, mascara and red lipstick smeared everywhere, admitting under the spell of tequila to whoever is around to listen that I don't want to be that girl.

this mess.

January 1ˢᵗ

Another year without him stings

and I'm still angry with my yesterdays

with the past that makes today

hard to breathe through.

It's dark tonight.

I search the sky for stars with no luck,
noticing only the sharp outlines that
appear to reach up to infinity,
shadows I've come to know as trees

There is no light but for the block writing
in front of the bus, no sound except for the robotic
female voice, which interrupts the incessant creaking
of the old metal parts to announce the next stop.

What if life informed us of what was next, I thought.

Wouldn't that be nice.

it used to work: running away.

but now grief has turned into a carry-on

and there's no leaving it behind.

I love him. I miss him.

every single day
and there's been many of them so far

but I don't want to carry this grief around any longer.

tell me,

where can I check-in
this burden?

I wish I could say that I felt him around me

but all I feel is an empty space inside

where his love used to live

and anger

that out of all the people in the world

he was the one

to leave.

I recline back
lungs full of smoke
heart filled with words I can't explain

who have I been these days?

it's strange not hearing his voice
forgetting his name

Please, Julia
sing me away
because tonight the skies are gray
dead without stars
the breeze has turned cold
Summer is gone
and I'm everything I've ever been.

All I have left are personal objects

and my memories

But what if one day his face fades away?

Will I have to freeze him in time?

What if I faded away already in his?

what if I just stay sad?

what if I stay this crazy, this numb,

this mad?

There we laid, side-by-side
limbs untouched
thinking of things to say
nothing too personal, of course
wouldn't want to get too close in this bed
Who are you? I want to ask
but stop myself, afraid he'd laugh,
and go on talking about minute details of my life instead,
wrapping my legs around his mid-sentence without
a second thought.
He feels tense. distant.
all the way over there, on the other side of the bed,
and I
accompanied yet still alone.

I wish he was here.

twist my body until

his memory

fades away

even if it's just for a few minutes

tonight

I need a stranger's arms

to hold me

together.

I wipe my tears away

with black leather gloves

I've become deaf and blind since he left

and transparent, too.

You should see how well

strangers can see

right through me

these days.

I just can't be a robot today.

and if I drown in this grief
then so be it.

I'm too sad
to be afraid
of death.

life pushes against you like a robber in the night

suddenly it shoves your face into a glass window

then demands you clean up the blood.

it's fucked up.

if only we had learned by now

how to not get caught

off guard.

I know what loss and grief and sorrow are, but I can't imagine
what it's like to realize you're dying. Is it a long, drawn out
epiphany, or does it take your entire body and world over in one
split second? Do you feel afraid for the unknown, or is it more like
relief? Does your life play out in parts, the memories connected
by flashing neurons strung together like pieces of clothing hanging
on a clothesline? Do you think of love? Do you wish for the warm
hands that touched you last? Do you pray, even if you don't
believe in God? And in that last breath, do you say whatever
words you have left out loud? And if you only have a second of life
to spare, how long does that second really seem to last?

what is it like to know you've reached the end and may
never again
                    get another beginning?

          so many questions without answers.

               if life is such an enigma,
                 can you imagine

                    death?

Merry Griefmas

My first Christmas with grief
was a mere three months after Paul passed away.
I didn't even have time to prepare,
I didn't even know such a thing was impossible yet then-
the pain was palpable,
cold and on the surface,
the loss starting to etch itself in my eyes and skin.
I barely remember it, though I do recall drinking my way through it
and at one point booking a tarot card reading. The reader
told me
you're trying your best to celebrate but you're depressed
to which I replied
no shit.
I went to have dinner at his parent's house on the 25th.
His mom was sick and after saying a cordial hello,
she spent the rest of the evening upstairs in her bedroom.
I didn't blame her.
It was unbearable to try to celebrate without him there.

My second Christmas with grief was better.
Mainly because I decided to skip the whole thing altogether.
I didn't send anyone gifts or Christmas cards. I wished everyone
a Merry Grinchmas and allowed myself the freedom to do as I
pleased with my feelings.
The only celebration was an intimate Christmas day spent with a
close friend and her immediate family in Fort Collins.
Christmas morning I woke up to snow and tears.
Merry White Griefmas.
But they didn't last all day, the snow and the tears- and they didn't
keep me from getting dressed and playing white elephant for the
first time with everyone else around the Christmas tree.
I felt loved.
It was nice.
But it all was still heavy. To me, anyways.
Probably because I was sad and sadness weighs a ton.
The thing about holidays is that they make the loss feel fresh all
over again,
it's like the scars are picked by the fingertips of
each encounter forced upon you,
each table you sit at surrounded by couples and family members,
and then there's that damn empty chair beside you,
the thought of the perfect gift you would've gotten him this year,
the memory of your very own Christmas tradition you

created together
brunch with a lot of Champagne and just a little bit of Santa,
just to say you celebrated it properly,
a balanced holiday affair, if you will;
Fresh tears start to flow with each Christmas card that arrives,
joy and love so clearly stamped on your friends' faces
it's so awful and conflicting
to feel so happy for them
and so sad
for me.
Self-pity comes easy then. Automatically, even.
But that was my second Christmas with grief.

On my third Christmas trying to befriend grief, I spent Christmas
Eve \at his parent's house, with his immediate family and growing
parts on his brother's side.
His mom and I were in high spirits.
We spent the day cooking up a feast and she ordered a
special Riesling
to go with dinner and she even baked a pie from scratch.
The house was decorated with wreaths, the Christmas tree hung
with vintage, curated ornaments his parents purchased in different
parts of the world,
a bowl of shelled nuts sat ready to be cracked near
the fireplace...
it was the image of a Scheffler Christmas.
It was still missing my favorite Scheffler of all, but there was joy
in that house that night,
and it was good to be able to actually feel a bit of that infamous
holiday spirit again.
Still no one talked about him.
We didn't want to remember his death on Christmas Eve or day.
The afternoon and evening of Christmas day was reserved for a
close group of friends, a night spent drinking and eating,
surrounded by good people.
I came home around 10:30 pm.
I was starting to feel worn out from all the holly jolly,
I could feel the sadness trying to seep through...
On the 26th, when my third Christmas with grief was supposed to
be over,
that's when the pain hit.
that's when the loss refused to be pushed aside any longer,
that's when it took over,
the wave I have come to know so well, knocking me down,
bending my body forwards,
making my bones heavy

and cold.
The next three days were a blur of takeout, hot tub dips, wine and beer, absolutely no exercise and twelve hours of sleep each night.
For dinner one night I ate a 12 inch pizza, 8 chocolate chip cookies, and half a pint of ice-cream.
I was desperately trying to make myself feel better, instinctively, in any way I knew how.
I couldn't talk to anyone.
I couldn't deal with anything.
I felt exhausted and sad and
alone.
Then, on the 29th,
I woke up and noticed I didn't immediately dread
the fact that I was alive.
I fed myself a healthy breakfast and sang some songs
and worked on the book, and took some pictures
to remind myself that I'm beautiful,
and cleaned out my closet, vacuumed the carpets,
drank a green juice for my afternoon snack,
witnessed a sunset from the hot tub
and thanked the heavens
that the holidays were almost over
and that today,
I was feeling better.
That meant the wave was passing,
that the worst had been felt,
that there was lightness of being to look forward to again.

I wouldn't say that my third Griefmas was easier than the ones prior,
but the days of sadness were fewer than those of happiness and when grief hit, I knew it was just another wave I had to ride through.

By then, I guess you could say,
I had a bit of experience
with grieving during the holidays.

I asked his mom if she was sleeping ok
and she shrugged her shoulders and said
yes, well, I exhaust myself
and just then I saw in her eyes
the unbearable pain of a mother
who had to bury her firstborn child
and I would like to say that
in that moment
my loss paled in comparison
but grief can't be measured,
it doesn't work that way-
it breaks hearts and
rips open chests
just the same.

loss is loss is loss is loss…

I am not giving up.

Some days
I just have to
give in
to grief.

TEARS FOR BREAKFAST

I have cried on the wooden floor
beside my dresser
my hands caressing the imperfect object with love
I have cried on the sofa,
my head buried in pillows as my mouth
gasped for air
and silence
I have cried on my bed
and on pages scribbled in black ink
my tears distorting my words
turning them into strange shapes-
this one, a boot
and that other one, a star
I have cried at my work desk, right in front
of the computer
and on the massage table so many times
now I have lost count
I have cried while riding my cruiser bike-
I can't help it
this mountain town used to be his alone
but now it has become mine.

Only mine.

I have cried on runs around the lake, while
chopping vegetables, and a handful of times
on first dates;
I have cried in the public bus,
most often behind dark sunglasses but
in front of strangers who will never
know my name-
which to me seems strange.
We have shared so many of my tears
together.

I have cried as I stood held in long embraces
by those who I can sense feel bad
for not having the right words to say-

they still haven't learned that
there are none.
I have cried as my face seemed to freeze
distorted with pain
and as my voice escaped from me in the shape
of a scream
the only sound I make when nothing
makes any sense
and not always, but sometimes
I try to muffle it so the neighbors don't think I'm insane
I feel that is ok-
the screams are not like the tears.
I have cried over both
life and death
and all the words I can no longer write
without hearing his name.

I have cried in planes and
in cities far away
enough to know that my tears will always
tag right along with me,
the saddest carry-on in history.
I have cried in the arms of my mother
a few times, but last time
was on top of a carpet covered in crumbs
which gave me a kind of sad comfort-
to know I wasn't the only thing broken
lying there.
I have cried until lashes fell out
enough of them for the entire world to make wishes with-
because the lashes
(it seems funny to say it now)
wanted nothing to do with
my tears
and I can still remember the first time I cried
in front of him
my hands on my face and then, his

I hid in shame because back then
I didn't understand
that tears are just feelings
I haven't learned how
to write down yet.

But I do know
how to cry
now.

I'm not tired of crying.

what tires me is not being able to

describe in words

all the feelings his death left behind

within me.

Some days

I'm still so sad

I gasp in between my tears

it's as if there are so many

that my breath

just can't keep up.

I spent the weekend in bed

one day
clutching my heart

the other
half numb, half dead.

endings come in all shapes and sizes

and still we will never have a say

in the one we end up

wearing.

Life and death dresses each of us as it desires

with the fabric of

change.

There are good days and bad days
but the last two
have been the latter
tea and words and tears
for breakfast
and a flood of memories my mind
hasn't remembered in a while
I want to be able to say more than just
I miss him when they sit beside me
concern flooding their eyes when they notice
my tear-stained face
but I have no words to explain
the insufferable longing in my heart except for
Saudade[1]
in the tongue of my motherland
suddenly comfort seems so distant
a dream my mind must have made up
to get me through today
and then tomorrow
and the day after that
because when life breaks you this way
you either live one day at a time
or die.

The in-betweens we create disappear
you learn there is only yes and no
I will and I won't
I want you or I don't.
good days and bad
but the last two have been the latter.

definitely.

Maybes no longer exist in my world.

---

1   Portuguese noun; A deep emotional state of melancholic longing for a
    person or thing that is absent.

there is a distinct sadness here
nestled in the space
his body used to take
loneliness
has settled in
found itself a home
on his side of the mattress,
in the crater in my chest,
and on his mom's new sheets
which I don't know how
still smell
just like him.

My cry has become effortless
the kind of cry that can be practiced in public places
without anyone ever noticing.

people are much too busy
to deal with tears these days, anyways.

it happens in the blink of an eye,
the stroke of a pen,
the notes of a song,
the spark of a memory, mostly
and instantly
it happens without hesitation or permission,
without giving me a chance to prepare
for the weight of sadness that comes
with every wave of grief

it's rude.
that's what it is.

for tears to show up
unannounced
after I have asked them so many times
to please stay away.

Tonight

It's just me

and the gaping hole

here in my chest.

I was born good at building home inside a box.

I was born good at organizing my insides so they look nice and neat for others.

I was born good at fighting the good fight and hiding the tears.

So I shouldn't be judged too harshly when I resort to doing those things. But let's talk about the weight of carrying the world on your shoulders.

Tell him you love your scars now that you have them, but it hurts knowing and remembering just how you got them. Tell him sometimes you wish you had been just one more privileged kid, too. Tell him you just want to be happy, too.

And so what if the challenges gave you strength?

So what if the battles gave you character?

How far can those two things get you these days anyways? Some of the strongest people are still having fights with God and praying for things to change.

You will survive because you have before.
Survival instinct is not asleep inside you any longer.

I'm pretty sure that's how these things go. But what do I really know.

I don't mind the idea of having a spirit animal
I just wish mine wasn't
a cockroach.

the snow came in early October

pushing the yellows and oranges
onto streets

down to the cold concrete

the sun hid behind gray clouds

and Autumn was nowhere to be found

with so much of Winter

all around.

some days when the sun is low
and the snow is high
I open my eyes
and just want to write
the day away

write until the tears start
and then stop
write to the fast then slow rhythm of my heart
write of all the hands I never held
and the ones I never will again,
write of the mountains I traded my oceans for,
write of the dreams I can no longer remember
and the heartaches I'm trying to forget,
write it all down
black ink on white paper
and then

      walk

         away.

how can you be sad in Paris? they ask

because they can't see the healing

that hides behind my sadness,

the romance in my tears.

I can't be who I was last time I stood here

the city stands still in its expansive gray as I change,

and then

change again.

I should get out and see the sun
but I stay in bed instead
trying to write
his death
away.

I cried my lashes off again last night

it felt exactly like the first time

my heart was ripped

out of me.

when something shattered breaks

it hurts just the same-

it just takes less time

for it to be put back together again

after the end.

how long until they see that my shoulders

also carry their own burden?

A punch to the stomach still hurts

even if they think me to be

the strong one,

the volunteer that carries
their world in my pocket.

woke up with a cherry bomb

fuzzy mornings are best

watching water fall like stardust

over flowers that will soon

shrivel and die

wishing the world always looked like it does through

my window,

like it does through hazel eyes.

I want to scream like I did

the day I found out he died

gasp for air

feel my heart aching inside

but it's Saturday,

two o'clock instead

and I'm still in bed

numb.

whose arms will hold me now?

what is the worth

of this breath

in my chest?

I wish it had been me instead.

He deserved much more from life

than just death.

He was like water evaporating
leaving me thirsty
as he disappeared into
thin air.

I'm running out of words to express

the emptiness his death left

in my chest.

everything hurts
down to the tippy toes of my soul
but they would never know
my red painted lips will always
whisper

I'm fine.

He would know better.

I have no words left to give

no piece of my heart

remains intact for me to share

so I dress myself in silence-

one layer for protection

and another for warmth.

Seeing my words

disappear like a ghost

almost makes me feel

safe.

I asked God why he didn't take me instead.

I couldn't move afterwards and spent the next two days in bed,

wasting this life away because the sun shining outside my window

no longer made any sense.

What if this is the type of pain
I can't write away?

I'm afraid of things that never scared me before he left.

182.5 to be exact

It's been 182 days of tears for breakfast
and words as a bedtime snack
and I'm still in this space where I can't understand
just how it is that someone you love
can disappear into thin air
but leave a giant hole in your chest.
It's been 182 days.
I still miss him
and then,
I miss him again.
I never asked that much of life
but death,
can't you please
bring my best friend back?

I've become just another tourist without plans

because nothing makes any sense

since the day he left.

I don't feel him here in these cobblestone streets.

I don't feel him anywhere.

so I walk around aimlessly

searching for him in all the places I know

he'll never be found again.

Him dying

felt like heavy snow

on the first day

of Spring.

I gave up today.

I gave in.

This is grief, I think.

There is no hiding from it.

He was a blanket for my bones,

the place I called home

now all I have is pen and paper

and my cold bones

for shelter.

open my eyes
to feel my body bare

nothing sits on my skin
but his scent

and in my lungs,
there's only his breath and smoke

on my lips,
the now fading taste of his tongue.

I used to love mornings alone.

Now I share them with the pieces of him

that he somehow

left here in my room.

It's more than just grief-

my heart feels as if it's missing a part of me

is that the part death takes when you two finally meet?

And what am I to do

with all this space loss left in my chest?

I can't control the tears

the fear of living life without him

and it's not that I want him to come back, necessarily

I'd rather just join him

wherever he is.

how much longer

until these tears run dry?

until the memories

don't cut into my heart

like a dagger,

until my feet get rest

and my heart

a bandage

to hold together

the parts life has scattered around

with the winds of change?

it's been a while

since I've spilled my guts

on blank pages.

emptiness

has settled where

he used to live.

everything is temporary

everything is passing

no one stays

but no one leaves

so I keep on

breathing in

yesterday.

I would like to feel strong

but right now

I'm just shattered

and all my words want to do

is find their way

to him.

I'm destroyed

every time I try to write about him

it's as if a nuclear bomb goes off inside

and all that's left

are the particles

of who I used to be.

It's been one year and seven months

since he left

and I don't cry every day like I used to anymore

but every now and then

I cry in an airplane, or at the grocery store

Just not to lose the habit

of sharing my tears with

strangers.

the light on the ceiling reflects my bedroom distorted, round-
shaped and contained within a globe.

this has been my world.

this bed, my fortress of pillows and sad songs
and words written in cursive.

if he could see me now, what would he think?

would he laugh at all the tragedy with me?

He always did.

He loved my storms.

sometimes I'm not sure whether to cry

over the words I can longer say or those

I'll never hear again.

in the printed version

they won't see the smudges

from the tears I cried

while I tried

to write my life away.

on writing a book.

how easy

the tears come

when I can't find

my words.

drunk with sleep

I've been spending my days

forcing these lucid dreams

to take shape,

forcing my words

to have some meaning

other than this

sadness

death left me with.

Endorphins race across my brains like a string quartet
pushing and pulling against each other until the noise becomes so
deafening that I find myself at peace.

only when everything inside me screams do I feel alive.

what is happiness but a certain balance of chemicals in our brain?
and if I'm unbalanced at least there's a warm embrace ready
when I need one these days.

For everything else
there's a doctor with pills.

For everything else
there is poetry and a dream.

sometimes he feels like a dream

and other times he's never been more real.

reality begins to blur with time-

am I better now, or

have I just grown accustomed

to his absence?

to this sadness?

It's dusk. You get in your bathing suit and go sit in the hot tub. You bring the new book you bought earlier but don't read it. Instead you sit there thinking about your dead ex-boyfriend and of how proud he would be if he could see how mature and stable and sober and responsible you have become. You start to cry because you miss him, because you feel lonely, because it's Saturday night and you wish you were somewhere else, doing something fun, not sitting here, alone.

But what if spilling tears in a hot tub is what your heart needs now? What if this is how you heal?

Maybe sitting in silence submerged in water without any substances in your system will finally give you the clarity you've been seeking. God knows you tried all the opposites already. God knows you've tried to outrun all these thoughts but you're never fast enough.

You recline your head back and look up at the now dark sky, sprinkled with stars. You try counting them and get to fifty, unsure if a plane or satellite snuck its way somewhere in there. Apparently you need glasses now. Still, you see three of the stars that make up the big dipper and that brings you comfort because you remember spotting them in Brazil as a child.

Maybe not that much has changed, after all.

When your skin folds in like an old woman's, you leave the hot tub, shower, and feed yourself popcorn and a frozen entree for dinner as you watch a series about an orphan girl called Anne who is all alone in the world.

It seems appropriate.

Around ten p.m., you drift off to sleep as Anne finds a family and falls in love in the background.

the pain grief gifts

can sometimes

cut too deep

for words.

so much to say

so much to write

but inside

sadness keeps hand

from connecting

to heart.

to have to continue smiling

both to and for

those left behind.

on the hardest part of death

how many more different ways are there
for one to say I miss you?

I'm not sure.

so I'll keep writing
until either I die or
run out of words.

I shoot a cold hard stare at my reflection on the window and
I swear,
sometimes I don't know who that person is.

I make her give me a half smile so the corners of her mouth don't
curve downwards like they naturally do; so she doesn't frown to
the world. My brother once pointed that out to me and I've been
smirking and half-smiling ever since

because when I leave this world, I want them to remember
me smiling.

Who are you?

I keep staring at her as I ask.

Sometimes I don't even recognize my own reflection.

Feeling my tired eyes, my shattered heart,
I see her sitting there, staring back at me
perfect on the outside
half-smiling as if everything is alright
and I'm almost convinced it is.

One look at her
and you'd believe it too.

everything is blue and white

icicles formed while trying to reach the sky

only to give up once they touched the ceiling

backwards

frozen and suspended

their only concern the heat of the sun

and I envy them lately

wishing I was momentarily hanging

upside down

just waiting for the perfect time

to melt.

Two words I no longer know how to answer:

Emergency Contact.

What he used to be but never will again
because my voice reached him without a need,
without a purpose or reason

Sometimes I just needed him to listen
but those weren't my emergencies then.

These are my emergencies now.

Sadness comes

without rhyme or reason
no logic will ever explain it's arrival

but wouldn't it be nice

if sadness gave a little warning

before crashing down on the heart like a giant hippopotamus?

maybe it still wouldn't be enough

but at least then it could find one a little prepared,

ready, even.

or as ready for sadness as one can get.

Wouldn't it be nice if sadness came

accompanied by a "heads up!"

before it found us,

maybe even happy?

why not?

it's not fair.

We don't stand a chance against the weight

of the sadness grief brings.

I want to leave behind

the tracking of time,
the last twelve months without him to

look at me and remind me

just what I'm capable of.

I have learned that letting go

isn't the same as forgetting

and when I turned to ashes I found that

Winter never lasts long enough

for me to forget

the time spent beside him

last Summer.

afternoons are best spent

with my head underwater

observing the gray sky

and barren trees

as a dead leaf

swings violently

from a spider's web.

I feel broken

but it's a different kind of dead that has decided to make itself at home inside

perhaps it's the ghost he never was

because he was more real than the fake smiles and the *I'm sorry* whispered by strangers who will soon forget his name

it is I who is left with all the memories
the I do's and I don'ts I never had a chance to say,
the laughs I still had to give,
the embraces I ran to after my longest days
and all of his favorite songs and words-
the smallest but most significant parts of him that made me fall in love
with his soul.

I carry them with me now.

I always will.

So keep your *"everything happens for a reason"* to yourself.

The simplest things can be the hardest sometimes

like seeing a picture of someone you used to love

months after they walked away or

apologizing for the words you didn't say;

like smiling to strangers when

you're dying inside

and seeing him and his big, innocent smile

in his mother's eyes-

It is the simple things that can kill us inside

so we complicate everything for the art of

staying alive.

He has been calling, texting me the usual *"how are you?"* that are always full of emptiness and devoid of care.

I never answer.

I can't.

My heart is already too shattered to be broken again.

no one understands me these days

and the only person I want to talk about it with is dead.

what to do

with all these thoughts

I keep

unsaid?

I'm all made up with nowhere to go

I said no to him and no

to the other one

I just want to be alone

and think about him

dying.

I haven't cried in two days
but it's been nine since he passed

I'm not sure what happened.

maybe something inside me shifted, or
maybe I heard his whisper from the other side
Please smile for me.

it hurts like hell

Discovering my things amidst his

makes me lose a part of myself

I know I'll never find again.

I want wine for breakfast
and I want it in bed.

It's Saturday, twelve p.m.
and I'm still in my pajamas,
bearing my soul to lined paper,
wishing he wasn't dead.

and I just have this feeling,
I just have this sense,
that today will be the kind of day
when it hurts too much to speak,
when it hurts too much to
get out of this room and
live.

I never hated Mondays before
but now Monday has become the day when I have to stop crying
and go be the person society needs me to be
when all I want is to stay in bed
and think about him
so I don't forget
anything.

I haven't forgotten

my dreams

completely

they just feel

too heavy

to think of

frequently

right now.

Isn't it amazing

how even after so many years,

so many changes,

so many losses and heartbreaks,

the tears never run dry?

They still always come.

LADY MEMORY

Welcome, lady memory

take a seat and tell me
what is it that you would like me to remember today?
the time we hiked three hours through a jungle in Costa Rica
or the last time I kissed his lips?
I can almost feel them again
purple and cold
my tears run free as you sit quietly
telling me all the stories I have been trying
to forget.

Pacific

Can you remember the last day we spent together?

You were jumping around in the Pacific, splashing water into the air with the force of your hands and getting deeper and deeper into the sea.

You were always afraid of everything, except of the ocean.

I loved you for that.

For I have always been afraid of nothing, except of the ocean

I had to learn early on about the strength of the currents.

So I stood there at the shore, safe enough from the raging sea to admire your childlike fearlessness and excitement over the towering waves,

your body trying to ride them, tame them in some way.

You didn't know then that you'd be dead the next day.

And now I'm so glad you swam deep, that you threw your body over those imposing waves and splashed around as if you had never before seen the sea

and looked at me with those eyes that always made me believe in everything.

I am just so glad you lived. Really lived.

Beyond my fears and yours, and the strength of the sea.

is there a way

to properly miss

someone?

it's like breaking while

keeping ourselves together.

it can't be done.

Remember the record player? The record player you bought two years after I had been telling you how much I wanted one. The same one you purchased two months after our love broke. Perhaps so you could keep a piece of me, there against the window, soaking up the stream of sunlight that used to dance across your wooden floors and my lap; perhaps just as bait to bring me back. Remember how you bought it broken, just to have it fixed? And how, even after months of playing Ryan Adams, I couldn't figure out for the life of me just how to turn it on? So I would plea for help: Sweets! My voice echoed along the corridors of your apartment. You always listened *and you always answered.* And so I learned to sing to you- *"And you and I were dancing in the dirty rain,"* my voice would carry the words and fill the space around us, and in the kitchen, with my feet placed on top of yours and my arms around your neck, that day we danced the first dance we'd never get to have.

you know the couple that starts dancing

long before anyone even has a chance

to hear the music?

that's who we were.

nothing between us started conventionally.

maybe that's why it stuck.

We found comfort in mutual rebellion
and grounding in the freedom

we gifted the other

to be exactly who we were.

there were no masks.

no trying too hard.

we just were.

and then

we were

in love.

There's something about this bus

that gives me my words.

Maybe it's the forced silence and darkness

that brings my thoughts to light and

plays my memories over right in front of me

as if they were streaming on a tiny television screen

Maybe it's because I took this route so many times

on so many nights

Sometimes just to hear him tell me that I would be alright.

And I would always text him on the way

I'll be there at 8. Please don't be late.

I'm starving, I'd say

and now there's still someone waiting for me on the other end of
the line.

But that someone is no longer him.

How can life change so much

yet not at all

from day to night?

the clarity I find

during my dark trips to Denver

is astounding.

There was this one time in Aspen-

we did yoga in the kitchen

and laughed as if we could

swallow the world

whole.

We were half sitting, half lying in bed, covered in blankets, a hot cup of coffee in hand, attempting to gather our energies to begin the day. Quietly he looked over at me from his side of the bed and said "*I love you.*" Just like that. I turned my face towards him and whispered "*I love you, too*" before bringing my lips to meet his.

Time seemed to stop then.

Everything that had mattered before, all the to-do's that couldn't wait, no longer made sense.

We were in love on a weekday.

Life would have to wait.

They say that there will come a day when I won't think of him.

it seems impossible.

he is everywhere.

his memory living within my walls.

With her body bent over mementos of old days, she inspected the reminders of a life that now felt as if it had belonged to someone else. This had been a traveling, passionate, wild woman, who had from an early age decided she would pursue her dreams- drink a *jus d'orange* at a quaint café in Paris, eat pizza in Venice, climb Bulgarian fortresses and attend New York Fashion Week. There was always a thirst for unknown destinations, different traditions to learn about, new cultures to embrace, something new to pull her out of the mundane, something different from the normal everyone else seemed to love so much.

But who was she now?

Who had she ever really been?

Sprawled across her bedroom floor, she felt pangs in her heart accompanied by the sudden, urgent need to be

reborn.

He was enough
just the way he was
the day he helped me plant my first sunflower
and as if speaking to the child inside me
he told me to not be scared for the worms
as I dug my shovel into the clumps of soil
putting all their lives in peril.

And I remember smiling at the fact that
we could yell at each other
and then spend the rest of the day's light
playing in the dirt
together.

Today I'm grateful that a year into our relationship you brought me "home" to Boulder to spend Thanksgiving with your family. I didn't know it then that this place would become my home after you left, that after you died I would spend my weekends roaming the mountains, my heart shattered and my legs running furiously so my mind could feel some peace and my heart heal the grief. Living in Boulder didn't make sense for so long for me ("where is the ocean? FIVE months of Winter? Why is everyone dressed like they're always going on a hike? And what the fuck is a Nalgene?!") I fought it so hard at the beginning, what with all my visions of what my life should be like back then. But today I'm so grateful that you pushed me out of my comfort zone, that you opened a whole new world, that you never put limits on my happiness. I can't imagine losing you and surviving anywhere else in the world. Holidays still don't mean much without you. I try, but I can't seem to find my holiday spirit. Maybe I left it with you when I kissed your cheek goodbye for the last time. Regardless, today is a day for being thankful, and having met you and the journey that ensued from our lives coming together is something I will forever be grateful for.

I never needed to be

his everything

because he always made me feel

much more than

just enough.

I don't know what to do with your birthday anymore. When I try to celebrate it and the life you lived, it makes your absence feel palpable, even more than it already is. How can you celebrate something death has tainted and taken away? So I try to celebrate you every day instead, to keep your memory alive in my heart and mind. But still once a year this day comes and it kicks me in the stomach, reminding me of how the World gained, and then lost, such a beautiful person.

I don't need to be reminded you're no longer here to eat carrot cake with me on your special day. I don't need to be reminded what age you would've been if you hadn't been taken. Every day I count the days without you. Every day I miss you as if you had just left. Every day I wish you were here. Every. Day. But on your birthday every year every day gets just a little bit harder to breathe through.

Wherever you are, I'm here wishing you had many years of life left to spend with me. I guess I should wish you happy birthday but what does that even mean now? I'm not sure. I just know that today I miss you a little harder than on any other day and am thankful that even though you were taken much too soon, you came into my life and changed it for the better until

the end of time.

a million thoughts a minute,

memories and those I have yet to make

commingle

and there,

right in the middle,

is him.

I used to scream from the front seat of his blue convertible

my arms sticking straight out of the car as if reaching for the sky

then I'd say *Come on, let's live!* and scream again

because it's Summer and right now I love him

just the way he is and he

loves me,

my screaming mouth and wild hair

blowing in the wind

forming into knots…

He loved the crazy in me.

And I loved him for that.

Some days

I still wish I could

see myself through his eyes

even if just once more

It's not enough

to know that once upon a time

he loved me

as much as he would ever love anyone

and the photographs that once spoke a thousand words

hide away quietly in boxes

waiting for the day

when the memory of his face

won't make me crumble inside.

We walked along the beach naked, our hands clasped together as we made our way back to the spot we had claimed on the sand. By now our area had been perfectly manicured by Paul, with one giant striped umbrella protecting two beach chairs and a cooler stocked with IPA beers and Whole Foods sandwiches. The weather was in the eighties as the sun began to dip below the horizon. It was a perfect Summer morning in San Diego.

The day seemed to languidly extend itself over us, stretching around us like the light now fading in the distance. Then the sun dipped below the line of the horizon quickly and delicately like a prima ballerina, and once there was just a sliver of light left across the sea, we grabbed our things and hiked the long way back to the parking lot from Black's Beach, a trip we had done many times that Summer.

Life may be the thing we do the longest if we're lucky, but in certain moments, it still feels as if we will never get enough time to live.

That was one of those moments.

One last sunset at a special spot on Earth we had made our own.

What do you think they'd want from you
in your leather and lace?

If only they undressed you enough to see
the parts of you I knew
then you'd really have them, sweets.

{I hear his voice so much sometimes}

It looked like a he, the shape I saw covered in layers of dirty clothing. I could've sworn I saw a beard, too. He laid on his side, one arm swung over the clump that laid next to him. His love. Under the streetlight, on the cold pavement, they laid together in a close embrace, with nothing between them and only each other to hold.

It was the loveliest sight I had seen in a while.

So I sat there, fingers widening out the blinds, tears filling my eyes. I was hypnotized by all the love I saw sprawled across the concrete, mixed with the drunks that walked by and stumbled out from nearby cabs. Everything those two people needed they were holding right there in their arms that night.

Simple. Honest. Beautiful.

I knew I was fortunate for seeing those two lovers from the comfort of the man-made fort with him. I was fortunate for witnessing so much love, and in turn, being reminded by the Universe that the greatest gift each one of us can have is the true, honest love of another.

On that night, and on all the other nights to come, two displaced people out on the streets found a home in each other.

And that's what love is: **home**.

That's what he was to me.

the moon is still blue

frozen, dangling in the sky,

waiting as the sun takes its time rising

inch by inch

chasing the glitter in the snow away

as light takes over yet another day

without him.

He

was the light to my darkness

and I

was the end of

his.

we should all be so lucky

I didn't lose him today

and still I lose him

every day

one day I forget the sound of his laugh

and the next the scent that settled

on the nape of his neck

Lately I lose parts of him like I lose eyelashes:

unwillingly and

everywhere

worst of all is I can't help it-

he's no longer mine to keep.

and over time the hardest part becomes

remembering the little things and

questioning whether

happiness will ever

feel the way it did with him again.

On the fourteenth of the fourth month on the calendar

his years of life would have turned to thirty-one

and I can't help but wish he were around

to tell me, like he did every year,

how much he disliked blowing off the flame of a candle

to celebrate something that to him never felt like
an accomplishment:

living another year of life,

breathing through another trip around the sun.

Normally I would say the joke's on him

but there's nothing funny about him being dead.

Those Fucking Facebook Memories

There he is, sitting beside me in a gray and white striped sweater, holding "America Again," a book by Stephen Colbert that I believe his mother gifted him. My hand is on his arm and we're both giving the person behind the camera slight smiles. I'm wearing a gray sweater with a white faux fur vest over it, and we look the image of happy; wholesome.

God we look so wholesome.

That was our first and last Christmas spent with his family in Boulder. Facebook tells me it was December 25th, 2012.

Five years isn't that long ago but I barely recognize the girl on the screen now. My hair in that photo is long, highlighted and blonde. At this time I hadn't yet started unraveling. I hadn't lost him or myself completely yet.

The heartbreaks and disappointments of the years to come, and then his loss, would lead me to crumble. The hair would be cut up to my jaw line (*why do we get so attached to hair anyways?*) and tattoos and piercings would start appearing steadily all over my skin. The colors in my wardrobe would dwindle down to white and black. But mostly black. No calm smile or hopeful eyes would stare back at the camera. Instead a deep sadness would settle in the same place everyone who has lost someone they love has- there in the eyes. And if you could look inside my chest, you would find a big empty space. If you could hold my bones in your hands, you would feel a heavy weight peculiar to grief.

Because that girl died when he did, too.

The girl staring at me from December 25th, 2012.

there are so many memories of him

that make me cry

I forget exactly which one

brought me to my knees

this time around.

"It was the best of times, it was the worst of times."

I finally understand that saying now, how life can break you just to reshape you- stronger now, wiser and aware of the beauty in my own breath and the importance of love.

And still.

The last 365 days without him to share my accomplishments and failures with have been the hardest. I have no regrets of things left unsaid like so many others because my words always belonged to him. And the ones I kept locked away he read in my eyes.

But what do I do with my words now?

I wish he were still here so I could tell him how much he changed my life, how his love gave me strength, how I finally learned to see myself through his eyes. But the only thing left to do now is remember, celebrate the years of life he had by drinking his favorite beer. And it all still doesn't make any sense. He was once a lover but forever my best friend, and amidst all the things I still don't understand was his unwavering faith in me and unconditional love. He was my soulmate and I was his, no matter what, we decided. He made me angry, he disappointed me at times, and he was awful with directions and going to bed instead of falling asleep on the couch. And yet. The mornings when he brought me coffee in bed and danced with me on top of his feet in the kitchen and hid from the world beneath piles of blankets in our own grown-up fort and held me close to his heart the first time I let him see me cry and told me it would all be alright... that's what I remember when I think of him now.

I remember him and I remember love.

But I still hate the fact that all I can do is remember. All I can do now is sit here, drinking his favorite beer and writing honest words he'll never read.

365 days later and I still feel everything.

You should've seen the sunrise this morning

for a moment I couldn't tell if what I was looking at was the ocean
or the sky, the clouds rolled in towards me, the shore above

like waves made of air, foamy with oxygen and an angel's breath

against the never-ending horizon

which stretched itself out to embrace the sun in all its colors of
yellow, blue, and lavender

Your seat would've been next to mine, my head on your shoulder

We would sit in the comfort of our silence and I'd write in my head
all the words I couldn't yet

say out loud or

bring to paper.

Dressed in white with bloodshot eyes, she climbed in bed, contorting her body around her sheets until she blended in with them, looking pure and serene. She lay still, moving only her lungs as she gasped for air, spilling tears until there were none left to give, no sobs, no feelings she didn't name or expressed; until he made her laugh.

She really needed that.
Because she was hurting and sometimes it got tiring to always play pretend to the world.

She just didn't know who to be. how to act. but she also didn't know how to be anyone else but herself. shattered in pieces, laying there, held together by French lace and his old, familiar voice.

You're the best person I have ever known. You are so strong.

If only she could be who he used to see.

Not this mess.

Not so broken and bare.

I want to remember him that way forever-

him on that night, the last we had together

his face lit up by a giant spotlight

as he stood on a checkered black & white dance floor

in his finest suit

gifting me his biggest grin

as his hand reached towards mine.

Collaboration Fest

It was just about this time last year. We were drinking beer and taking home the free glasses they were handing out to the horde of lushes surrounding us. *One per person*, they said. But we took home five. Probably because I never liked rules and he was always so good at breaking them. I wouldn't say we were a match made in hell, necessarily. But there was nothing angelic about us either.

We were wild together.

And I loved him for that.

When people ask me what

he was for me

I find myself without words-

what is the term for strength and shelter and

the purest form of love?

everything

His body may be gone but he's still here-

in the wood of my dresser, the ring of my cruiser bike's bell,
in butterfly prints and photos hanging from my walls, in his brother's
smirk and in his mother's eyes, in his perfectly written calligraphy
on old birthday cards; he's on the trail to the top of the mountain
and on the breeze that blows my hair around; he's the cold glass
of beer on a beautiful Friday in the Fall and the black dots on my
set of dominos carved from stone.

How could he be anywhere else?

Even though he died he certainly didn't die to me.

His memory is *here,* his love alive in my heart.

it's strange.

him not being here and yet

being everywhere.

It's the way it'll be from now on-

I'll see him not at all but often

and miss him

just the same.

London is gray

everyone wears black

as if mourning for the sun.

naturally I feel right at home.

I keep thinking of him in his checkered scarf

wondering: would he stop and stare at doors with me?

would he walk these streets

just to get lost

with me?

Birthdays

Although he is no longer around to
grow old with me
there won't be a year when I grow old
without him.

Months go by,

weeks,

days,

hours...

I count the time as I search for him in the eyes of a passerby

and find nothing but memories

that feel as though they belonged to someone else

in a different life,

in a different time.

It's the good memories I try to remember now-

he didn't live long enough

but he sure as hell

made his breath

count.

It's strange how memories fade.

where do they go when they leave?

up above, beyond the clouds? Or do they just hang down below instead?

underneath the dirt of our dirty soles, our tired souls...

who can no longer remember the curve of smiles, the scents left behind in the imaginary trail our bodies made?

to where exactly do our memories fade? and who can say how fast?

why are some ghosts of our pasts still here and others long gone

far away enough from our minds that we no longer know who's alive and who's really dead.

No, not anymore. Not these days.

Where do memories go when they fade?

and what if they stayed instead?

The distinction between past, present, and future is only a stubbornly persistent illusion.

I find myself staring out into the endless ocean, looking right at the bright blue line that divides sea and sky. I remember the past year as parts that are so enjoined with the present that I confuse myself.

We are told our whole lives not to dwell in the past. But if there is no distinction between past, present, and future, then to forget the past is to simply forget ourselves. Forget who we are.

So when I sit lazily by the sea, I dive right into my memories- all the good ones I keep stored in a little treasure box in my brain. I pull them out as if trying on a new dress, turning them this way and that as I let them teach me who I've been. Sometimes during this process tears that weren't spilled when they should have been come find their place on my cheeks.

And it's wonderful to be alone with my memories and the sea. It's wonderful to see time as continuous and past events as ones that were never, and will never, be kept solely in the past. They are here on these waves, on the hot sand, under the shade of the umbrella and over the pedestrian walkway. His name is written with seashells on the shore, his face sculpted in the clouds, and his voice a quiet whisper I hear in every crashing wave.

POST TENEBRAS
LUX

the good part of him leaving this world
is the desire it has given me
to set it on fire.

the silver lining of death

This weekend I drove to my new house, the new place I hope will feel like home. I drove past the three jobs I held in a little less than three years, past the building where I used to collect food stamps, past all the streets once unknown but now so familiar, past all the bus stops where I waited, with the rain, with the sunshine, in the snow, in the wind, for the future I dreamed of to catch up with my heart. *"Look, you're here!"* I said to myself, at the first step of the new beginning you've been wishing for and the last you take to leave the past behind for good.

It's bittersweet to walk away. After all, how fast is too fast to be able to be happy again without guilt? Moving forward is hard to do without wanting to bring a carry-on. You know, just in case. But what is it exactly that has become so worth holding on to? Staying in a moment, living in a memory that is long gone is harder to do. It's heartbreaking, and it is so every single day when you cling. So let go and let your lips smile as if you have never known tears before. You have already fought the battle, and look, you survived!

Now it's time to thrive.

Now it's time to live.

what used to be stillness has become constant movement

I see so many blue skies without clouds these days

and I've learned that in time

everything fades

everything changes

everything dies

just to then grow again

everything flows right along

so shouldn't I?

the letting go will never become the forgetting

and of my entire heart

there will always be a part

that belongs to him

and him

alone.

Today I read a book for three hours, ate breakfast in bed, went boxing, stood upside down in a headstand for a few breaths, said a prayer while confronting and asking God for all the deepest desires of my heart, sat in a hot tub until my fingertips turned wrinkly and my mind quiet, vacuumed the carpets, did laundry, scrubbed the toilet, wiped down the counters, fed myself healthy meals, dusted off the guitar and played a couple of songs I wrote a few years ago (and still remember!), watered all three of my plants (that are still alive!), discussed past life regression with my roommates in the kitchen while making breakfast, spent $3 at a thrift store on two tiny wine glasses and a glass planter, and came to the realization that I am so abundant and supported in my life and that all is well. Just as it is.

All is well.

What a wonderful feeling to feel.

I haven't been writing lately-

It's not that I don't have the words

I just don't need them these days.

My life has become a hammock
that sways back and forth
on top of the mountain
I worked so hard to climb.

Is this the reward for not giving up?

I reach the peak
and there it is-

peace.

Sweet sunshine

seep through my skin and settle

deep down into my heart

fill it with the hope of Spring and the promise

of budding trees and blossoming flowers

remind it that everything has a cycle

a beginning and an end

and that rebirth always follows death

again and again and again

teach it to be strong and unwavering

just like you are-

darkness may come

but it always bows down

to the light.

You stop dating assholes and start dating yourself. You go to the movies on half-day Tuesdays and learn that a bottle of red wine and a bag of popcorn make excellent companions. On the weekends you cook yourself breakfast, eat in bed, and then lounge around and read for a bit before going on a lovely hike. You get a second job driving for Lyft for a few months so you can go on a trip to see the ocean. You work and work and work and pay all your bills and two credit cards off in three months, and then you finally book a solo trip to a fishing village off the coast of Puerto Vallarta. You never stop believing things will get better. Then suddenly life starts falling in place nicely together and Sunday mornings are spent reading a book about death while your boyfriend makes you pancakes. You remember the days when you dreamt this up in your head, when you tried to envision it with your mind's eye. You had to leave so much behind to get here. But see how great lightness feels?

See how nice it is, this future you built?

You are doing just fine, kid.

Go with the flow and just let it be.

This is happy.

I talk a lot about darkness because I have had to learn to treat it as an old friend of mine. But don't be mistaken-there's a lot of light in my life, too.

Light in people and faces, places and spaces, light that comes suddenly and inundates my entire world in a second's time. Light that arrives in the shape of clouds, of $20 dollar bills found on a deserted staircase, light that surrounds me after being filtered through newborn green leaves. Light. So much light. The sun rises over my bedroom window and I lay beneath the covers and notice the golden streams of light dancing- first across my white comforter and then over my face, eventually settling down to make home in my eyes. Sparkling light, new and bright. Virginal light- the kind that carries no shadows or hint of darkness. Because if there's one thing I learned walking through it, is that darkness ends. Always. And then there's all the light. And aren't you glad you stuck around to see it? You held on for all this light. Of course you can see it down to its photons. It is only natural.

Just because I have befriended darkness doesn't mean I can no longer speak of the light. The light in his eyes when he tells me he loves me. And means it. The light in her eyes when she tells me I'm still her favorite person. We both lost so much when he passed, it only makes sense we rebuild our lives together. Brick by brick our love strengthening our breath, giving wind to our feet. Drenched in the light streaming through the tall windows of the bar nearby, grabbing drinks and spilling quiet, reluctant tears as we affirm to each other in silence that we are doing alright.

Light.

I live in it. I just dabble in darkness sometimes. Perhaps just so as not to lose the habit. We have come such a long way, after all. Maybe that's the biggest gift I've gotten out of all the loss:

to be able to co-exist in both darkness and light and find beauty in it all.

You've outgrown your tears

here you are,

sitting cross legged on a rock

looking down from the top of the mountain

realizing just how far you have come

here you are,

stomping your fears away

on the glittered muddy path

one foot after the other

you will cry if you must

but you will never

stop.

I have gained a lot from my loss.

clouds float by and dissipate

one into the other

almost bare branches

hold on to dead leaves

as if they have forgotten

the promise of Spring

change is necessary

I want to remind them

to reach out and shake off all those leaves

and watch them fall to the ground,

one by one kissing their final resting place

but I am not Father Time

and it is beyond my power to force transformation

on trees and people and my heart

if all are not ready yet.

so I sit and watch clouds dissipate

one into the other

leaving a faint trace of themselves behind

before taking on a new shape and

embarking on a new path.

how crazy it is

to be able to carry

so much love and

so much loss

in this one heart

of mine.

been spending more time than usual

listening to the familiar

coming home to myself

healing the scabs instead of picking them;

been keeping my words on lips

and lined pages and investing

in the power of my lungs and strength

of my heart;

been keeping my tears safe

and my mind wild,

been living the love I have yet to have

and holding on to the hope that everything that has been

precedes even better days.

How amazing-

to live beyond the grief
and broken smiles
and have enough strength left
to write about it.

It wasn't too long ago when the thought of getting out of bed felt incredibly difficult, when I'd have tears for breakfast and sit in the dark paralyzed and numb on a beautiful sunny day. It wasn't too long ago when even walking took every ounce of strength I had left, when my muscles ached with grief, when happiness felt like a distant dream that would never come. Funny how things change, how you learn to find the strength you never even knew you had. It doesn't happen overnight but slowly getting up becomes a little easier, you start walking farther, until one day walking is no longer enough. So you run. You don't know why, maybe you start just so you can hear the drum of your heartbeat in your ears, reminding you that you're still here. You're still alive. And it's clear to you then what an incredible blessing that is. Running slowly starts changing from torture to possibility, from exercise to therapy. You put one foot in front of the other and you accept the challenge life has given you with death and you start to challenge it right back. Watch me run up these mountains, watch me leave grief in the dust, watch me grow and succeed, watch me become the person I've always wanted to love and be. Watch me become free.

This is how I went from hating running to letting it heal me.

I don't know when it happened

my tears switched from despair
to pure joy under the falling snow
and somehow these mountains
have become my own
and his arms
home.

lucky year number 3

his memory no longer stings

like it once used to

the pain

surface level now

the loss no longer

debilitating

perhaps that's the most beautiful thing about love-

how it always finds a place

to nestle itself into

as it turns dark spaces

into halos.

I had to reteach myself how to dream.

I should be grateful I realized I had forgotten.

But what to do of the dreams come true?

Is now the time to dream up some more?

I would say it's a shame to be getting everything I wanted

but then again, I'm the one

living my dreams.

And it's hard to feel sad when you're happy.

But isn't it weird how easy it is to get sad about how happy
you are?

I put all my favorite books on top of my bed.

our bed.

The plural has felt a little strange lately,

like when the cashier at the liquor store

knows your name.

Still I undress my soul

hoping he's able to spot magic

in scars and bare bones.

how many crazy dreams

I have shared with a pen and paper,

how many ideas and plans have seen

perfectly blank pages,

how many loves I have invented,

how many ghosts I have chased away

with the stroke of my pen

how many dead I have risen,

how many different lives I have lived,

how many hearts I have broken,

how many lies I have told myself to believe,

how many tears I have caused, but also joy

because words become feelings

when feelings won't do

but today I write love into life

and hope in the darkness

because that is what a writer can do.

You pour yourself a drink and sit outside in the sunshine to enjoy it. It is still Spring. But on days like today, when the sun is high in the sky and burning hot and bright, you can taste Summer in the air. Yesterday when he had to say goodbye after spending four nights by your side he pulled your hand away from all the to-do's and slow-danced with you in the kitchen before leaving. Your life isn't necessarily easy, but it's slowly becoming everything you dreamt it could be.

Not too long ago...

You almost never think about it now. At least not like you used to. The history of your footsteps only matter because they have brought you here, to this morning, this new day, this moment when you look into his eyes and you know:

This is it.

This is worth living for.

This is love.

Maybe now is the time to pursue destiny

and not stay stuck in the comfortable
maybe this is when I start a new chapter, or maybe

it's an entire book.

Maybe endings are actually beginnings

and heartbreaks chances for healing.

Maybe I'm not walking away but walking towards

forwards, moving closer to happiness

than I've ever been.

Maybe mind can remind heart of reality

and maybe the only way to move on

is to move

through it.

for the first time in my life
I'm learning what it's like
to have stability
and I had no idea
that I could feel so free
with both feet
firmly planted
on the ground.

If I had to choose between Mother Nature and humans these days, I would definitely choose the former. Something about the only sound out on the trails being the drum of my heartbeat and a bird's song makes me feel alive and whole. Mother Nature doesn't ask questions, she doesn't judge, but she does speak- gently, softly if you pay attention. A butterfly landed on my hand as I sat writing about death
and I thought how wonderful!
Rebirth and transformation materialized, come alive on the tip of my finger.
It told me I'm never truly alone then flew away, as if to teach me a lesson.
They say you should befriend loneliness, so what is so wrong about making it your closest friend?

There's a trail brimming with life out in the world that I've befriended,
and Autumn is just beginning as the old me is ending.

I'm shedding my skin

every day I discover a new piece of me

as I lose another part

I thought I would always be.

I like the version of me I'm becoming

she seems to be more me

than all the me's in the past

I like the fire in her belly

and the power in her voice

I like that she sets boundaries

and that she's fiercely independent

and thirsty for all the magic in life

I like the me I get to be now

after leaving so many parts of me

in the past.

It's been days of spending time with friends under both the sun and stars, days of long morning hikes and afternoon barbecues, days of cold drinks drank in patios, days of sitting on the rail of a porch and dreaming straight through sunset, days of talking and those of not speaking a word, days when I can't help but feel love explode in my chest as I ride my cruiser bike past the mountains that have taught me so much about endurance and the price to pay for strength.

isn't it funny how things change?

Summer comes and I forget all about Winter, about the times spent screaming into pillows and the days when even the sun couldn't pull me out of bed.

So much darkness and despair.

But Summer comes and I forget.

I had to learn to love myself
I had to learn to water my own garden
and look how tall my wildflowers have grown!

I had to learn to stand on my own two feet
and count on my fingers
the few shoulders I could lean on
when my legs got much too tired to carry me through.

I had to learn to stay still
even with wings ready to fly
and to live a life
measured by the number of my smiles
and not commas on a paycheck;
to speak new languages,
and train my tongue to twist and touch the roof of my mouth
this way and that

But I also had to unlearn
the logical linear thinking they wanted me to have
and the tendency to so easily give my heart away
Someone taught me to build these walls-
they weren't always here.
I once believed in a forever kind of love;
a happy ending;
and it's not that I don't still wear my rose-colored glasses
(at least occasionally)
I am just wary of where I wear them to now;
of who I wear them around.

and still
there's much to learn
and unlearn
because just when you think life is through
is the moment when it really begins.

And I have had to learn that, too.

Walking away

hello old friend

somehow I knew we'd end up here.

Letting go is an art

and each time I'm called to the canvas

I keep getting better

shedding the past and parts of myself

like an artist with colors,

a goodbye in each

brush stroke.

I'm filling in my bones

growing past the shell

and shadows

my skin taut with

strength and hope

my mind wild with dreams

and my heart

foolishly

in love.

loving him splits me right in two-
the person I wish I was
and the person I actually am.
Teach me how to face the past
while embracing the present
Tell me how to heal
these wounds I uncovered
when my heart
started beating
for him.

Now, they will never tell you this but you have to watch out in life so as not to trip on the mountain of disappointments that grows taller with each year; with each ending of the beginnings we have had to live through; with every shoe that dropped to meet the other.

Personally I like to leave mine in a corner somewhere- that way I know I won't trip on it and fall on my face.

Not again, anyways.

It seems to work. I'm still here.

Unscathed.

Before I had my own four walls
there were those who had theirs

and welcomed me in,

gave me a place to lay my head and rest my heart.

I had no clue back then what an extraordinary gift that was –

I took their kindness for granted

and disappeared without a trace

when my mind made the four walls close in on me

and left me wishing for death.

But when four walls become home

and strangers become family

walking away is always temporary.

So like the prodigal son I returned,

arms open this time,

desperately trying to replace the loss in my heart

with love.

And as soon as I was embraced and welcomed back,

I regretted all the time I wasted

closing myself off to the support I always needed

but didn't' know how to ask for.

tell me that I've seen the worst

tell me that from now on things will stay the same

except for the few

that still need to change

tell me there's safety in growing roots

and tell me you will lay down next to me

on days when it gets too hard to stand.

There is a quiet sadness in goodbye, in the *see you later* in life that are always justified but never guaranteed. and yet

I pack my bags and don't look back, my eyes focused on the infinite line of the horizon, searching for what's ahead without regretting the tears left behind

on cobblestone streets and plain white sheets, on airplane seats and empty rooms where many times I've found myself alone but never lonely.

because sadness is what you make of it.

the question of self-pity.

he kisses my wounds

and blesses my scars

running his fingers on the raw spaces

still within me with care

as if he knew

all I needed to heal

and begin anew

was this love.

his love.

I'm not broken I'm just

shattered

I can piece myself

back together.

thankyouverymuch

I don't say it to anyone

but I love trees so much

because I know what it's like

to feel dead for so long

and then suddenly be

brimming with

life.

It's interesting to experience everything in my body protecting me from myself, turning open wounds into scars in the process.

Is this how we heal? by forgetting? or is it by not remembering?

Because now I'm certain they aren't the same thing.

the breeze is slowly turning

a little bit cooler every day

it's the same as it was last year except

everything

       has

          changed.

The humming of the refrigerator has become my favorite sound.

It's Sunday and we're up before the sun, laying side by side with our backs flat on the shaggy carpet in the living room. Blankets cover our bodies. I place a sleep mask over my eyes as he opts for his blue bandanna. We breathe deeply, our arms intertwined and hands clasped. I try to listen to every sound, but it is so early the rest of the world is still sleeping. There's just the humming of the refrigerator and the swooshing of our breaths filling the space around us. In and out. With my third eye I see flashes of light and a never-ending night sky. And when the time comes to fully return to my senses and this body in this world, I will see a sky colored in pink, purple, and orange, and he will still be wrapped up tight in a blanket and I will look back at him and wonder how it is that the sight of him can rival a sunrise.

I live for these little moments when I can feel so full and whole and safe.

For slow Sundays and sunrises and plans of forts while drinking coffee and making pancakes. For the everyday magic and the humming of the refrigerator that keeps me believing life is worth living.

Love is worth giving.

I'm learning to give room

to the in-between
spaces

within me.

I cross two things off my to-do list

two out of seven

then pat myself on the back
not bad for a Monday, pal.

those five other things can wait.

until I'm done waking slowly, rising languidly, letting life take my body and soul over again inch by inch, breath by breath,

until my limbs have collapsed on the floor, sweaty, exhausted, sore and alive

all at once,

and my mouth has drank and sung and kissed

until I've listed everything I'm grateful for to myself and whoever else might be listening, counting as the sun rises the many blessings found in the mere fact of being alive.

life.

live it.

Don't waste it with the mechanics, the automatics.

The joy is in the journey

don't you forget it.

sana sana colita de rana

by the time I met him

I was so used to

kissing my own wounds

that I started to kiss his

without a second

thought.

He would have liked the woman he saw if he had seen me last night. My skin sun-kissed, hips swaying back and forth to the rhythm I learned in the only home I've known, to the songs I used to spend hours dancing to alone on the patio on days when the sun shone too hot and there was no one around to talk to.

He would've liked the way my mouth molded over the notes, my tongue dancing, vocal chords ringing, my spine standing strong and upright. He would've appreciated my efforts at human connection sent to the crowd over the twisted microphone wires, and afterwards, I'm certain he would've declared that I had been born for the stage.

He was, after all, my biggest fan.

He would've sat right in the first row but he would've stood up to dance, even if his feet never did quite learn all the right steps to take.

That's what he had me for, after all.

He would've liked what I have done with this life I realized I took for granted when he died.

Why have I wasted so much time?

I have learned to ask myself the hard questions, even if I don't have answers to so many of them.

yet.

What I do know is that it is not enough to just breathe and pay the bills and kiss new lips every now and then. Not anymore.

He would be proud of the woman I have become.

If he could only see me now.

Sanity

lemon haze and this creek
the sun's heat on my naked skin

My limbs on the breathing earth

the cool breeze a tease of the Winter that is to come.

Here,

peace.

silence.

Hush hush now

be who you are and worry not about the aren'ts

The leaves whisper the name they have given me and

with my head and body leaned against an old, wise tree

I sit

and I am still

Still.

there is a rush of words

and then peace and quiet

silence and fulfillment

but they are still here, hiding beneath my tongue,

just waiting for my heart to

pump them up and out

onto the page.

RED ROCKS

I'm waiting to feel what I felt last year

him and I here

and now

just me.

the lights, the sounds, the rocks, the moon...

everything stayed

except for him.

and it may be that I'm standing in the same place

again but I'm not

who I used to be anymore.

Nothing is.

You lose people.

Sometimes to death
and other times not.
You lose them in coffee shops and
through telephone wires
and sometimes you even lose them
in bed.

You lose people
before they even know it,
at times you can lose them in the most ordinary moments-
during the walk to the store,
while waiting in line at the bank,
and in the shower you take before heading into work.

You lose people.
But the ones worth keeping
will always find their way back to you somehow.

You lose people.
But sometimes when you lose someone
you also find yourself.

Loss can be a win
if you let it.

You lose people
and other times people lose you.

and so it goes, round and round,
losing and winning join forces
and in the end the only thing that matters
is that you don't ever
lose *yourself*.

GROWING PAINS

There is a heaviness in my chest, a sadness disguised as melancholy, a lingering sense that nothing that has been will ever be again. I miss my yesterdays, even the ones that weren't so great. Funny how memories sting when they leave. But I'm breathing in hope and feeding on wishes, searching for the silver lining in every dark cloud above me, hoping for days when my feet won't feel so heavy, so tired from all the climbing and trudging through thorns that life has made me do.

I smile often. I speak encouraging words. But inside my heart aches more than my mouth will ever dare admit. Alone with my thoughts is when I find my truth, when I sense just how far along I've come in piecing myself back together.

So am I strong now?

Yes.

But sometimes I wish life hadn't forced me into strength.

Sometimes I wish I could've just stayed the same.

Stayed average.

Stayed safe.

sometimes it feels as if the snow

will never melt away

but then you wake up one day

the sun is shining

birds are chirping

and all of a sudden

it's the first day of Spring.

If I had to pick one word to describe me

I'd choose

raw

unprocessed, unedited,

tender but fervent

never diluted

and always

strong.

strange

how the older you get

the more things seem to lose sense

time becomes a blur

and you can't understand

what it was that came

before or after

the moment that made you

who you are

today.

I'm not crumbling any longer

I've been gluing myself back together

with this grief, transmuting my tears

into stitches holding up the

shattered parts of me.

I was never whole and perhaps I will never be.

But today I am more *me* than I have ever been.

I sit in the sun and hear the birds sing

and it's all beautiful

it's all enough

just as it is.

if you had told me a year or two ago

that I would fall in love

and feel true joy again soon,

I would have laughed in your face.

Turns out life is full of surprises too,

it's not just death.

the funny thing about death

is how it suddenly makes you

see life exactly

for what it is.

I feel change in the air

as if it were incoming rain, a barely-there sprinkling

slowly building into a beautiful storm

nothing ever stays the same

and that makes saying goodbye to yesterday

even more difficult

I feel him around now and then,

pushing me forward,

reminding me of the person he saw

the person I've grown into.

But happiness can be scary if you've never really known it,

misery will always be more comfortable if you were forced to
befriend it.

Switching tears for smiles is frightening

when you don't know if you can trust

life to bring you joy again

and for you to be able to keep it

this time around.

It started pouring rain

I sought shelter underneath a giant mushroom

then remembered I had an umbrella

still

I stood staring at the sky

as raindrops formed puddles around my feet

fantasizing about the rain

washing everything away.

clean slate.

This is who I am these days.

funny

how some days feel

like the end of the world

and others

like just the beginning

two

are far too many
goodbyes

to have to say.

He stood naked between sand and sea, arms extended out in the shape of a cross while the wind threw the few hairs left on his head back and forth. I couldn't see his face, but I imagined his eyes closed, his mouth parted and shaped in a slight smile as he exhaled all the frustrations of his life out in one big breath. I let out a quick, quiet little laugh that could have been mistaken for a sense of my own superiority. But down below my still ringing vocal chords was a burning desire to become that man; to wear nothing but the wind on my skin as God intended and leave all that weighed me down on that spot in the sand.

And then there are days that feel magical
the notes in the wind sway your body back and forth and you
can't tell anymore
what's driving what

It's just you. In this world of seven billion.

Just you.

So you close your eyes to see what they can't
and all of a sudden
you're safe.

You're ok.

I light the candles unapologetically

for no one and

everyone that matters

for the love lost

and battles won

for Spring after Winter

and for the feeling

of coming

home.

I wish I could say that grief feels distant

a year later but the waves

still come.

the only difference is that now

I know how to hold my breath

when my head goes under

so that grief no longer drowns me

in pain.

love knocked on my door

so I let love in

It said it was here to take over

from death

and apologized

for being so late.

ONE HEART

it may be

that we have lost much

but we have not lost ourselves

our empty spaces

will come together

to form a home;

one heart.

We hope for a day when relief will come, pray we get a gift from life instead of another taking from death. But what if that day never arrives? What if, over time, we lose hope? What if one day, that hard day, is one we choose not to fight through?

Giving up doesn't happen overnight.

It takes time to slowly beat a human into hopelessness and despair.

If we could only have a string of days adorned with joy and love- that would be enough to keep the heart beating through the eventual dark days to come.

Because when you're forced into darkness, sometimes you need someone to come inside and crack a window open, let hope and light in.

So many times others have done that for me.

Now let me do it for you.

What I wish they had told me about losing someone you love is
that you'll never be the same again. You will finally understand
the illusion of time- how some days feel as though they'll never
end, and others feel like a brand-new beginning. Many a sad
memory will come to pay you a visit. You will suddenly remember
the first kiss again. And then, the last. For a few months you will act
unlike yourself just so you can feel alive again. You won't be able
to stand that dull, numb sensation taking over the space where
your heart used to be. You learn death doesn't just take your
loved one away and leaves after that. No. Death hangs around.
It stays. It becomes a part of who you are now. For better or for
worse. Some days it makes you passionate about things you never
even noticed before, like the white trail clouds leave behind. And
others, it makes you never want to see a blue sky again. It's messy
and disorienting and heartbreakingly painful. At first. And then,
always. It doesn't get any better with time like they say either. You
just learn to live with it; to befriend it and let it in. And then it never
leaves. You let it take over so the past can die and stay behind
and that's how you learn to live again. That is the time of your
rebirth. Your heart and soul will grow so big that one day you stop
being who you were and you become love. so let the tears come.
let them wash away the pain.

(this is how you grow)

just as easy as the tears come
so will the smiles.

hold on.

It is not always easy- climbing your way to the top. Walking away from comfort or darkness, or both. Sometimes you trip on the way or run out of breath. Sometimes you get so tired. It would be so much easier to just give up. But you never do. You somehow put one foot after the other, live one day and then another, until you find yourself at the top and realize just how far you have come. You look down and lose your breath all over again but this time it's different- a wave of joy steals your breath away instead of the despair you used to know so well. And suddenly you can't help but stand there, letting your bones soak in all the beauty, peace, and fulfillment, thanking the universe for the path that brought you here, no matter how difficult it was.

In the end, there were no shortcuts. Because the view at the top isn't for everyone. It's for those with strong hearts and fire in their lungs.

It's for you.

It's for me.

We just have to keep climbing.

the in-betweens of life

riddled with uncertainty

can often be the hardest

to get through.

but you will.

You've come far enough for your legs

to keep on pushing, even if

your heart still drags a little behind

in the past.

they say you should hang upside down,

get a new perspective and all,
but up is still up and down is still down

when you're upside down

and no matter what they would like to think

you're still in the same exact place you were

the day death became your friend.

and yet.

you are also here.

Here at the end of the beginning you once had

and at the beginning of the end that you were given

and you made it through another day.

Sometimes you have to let that be enough.

Some days even when the words come

you must hold them back-

not everyone deserves to know

how often your heart

breaks.

What I've learned from the mountains

no matter how tired your legs or

how heavy your heart

you have to keep moving forward

carrying in one foot hope

and in the other one

strength.

There is no formula for healing and no shortcuts on your way to growth.

Take the long road but
walk it *your way*.

For the dark corners you have learned to embrace
and the soft spaces you still keep;
for the fragile strength that has carried you through
and the bravery you have shown
when you stared death in the face
and chose instead
to live.
to love.

For the decision you make
day after day
to keep hope within reach
and let go of grief,
for the honest tears you've shed
so openly with yourself
and the mountains you climbed
on your way
to peace;

For your eyes and lips
and ears and fingertips
and hot breath in your lungs
for staying present through it all;
For what was
what is
and what's yet to come.
for growth.

For the voice you birthed from the pain
and for the courage you've found to walk away
and let the past
die for good.
For Spring after Winter.
For the light in the darkness.
For rebirth.
For you.

It's not easy-

reaching darkness

just to later walk out of it

I just hope that the light you have

is bright enough to bring you back

I hope you don't forget that

none of that darkness

belongs to you

or is yours to keep

Treat it as a brief encounter

a first date you never want to see again

get what you need

and leave it just where it is:

behind you

a story of your survival

a testament of your strength.

When you finally start getting everything you want, be brave enough to say yes and humble enough to say

thank you.

You don't have to move

past the pain-

You just need to learn

to let it pass

through

you.

I know some days you feel like heavy snow on the first day of Spring. when you come down you crash hard and unexpectedly. but be what you are. who you need to be. soon the sun will shine and chase your storms away.

(as it always does)

don't let them tell you how to feel. the ground is still beneath their feet. how could they possibly understand

what   you   need.

turn your gaze inwards

see how the ground beneath beckons?

settle down and learn from the earth-

realize that you will never outgrow heartache

until you tend to your

own roots

first.

you don't need the

empty spaces

in you

filled

you just need them

             embraced.

lessons from death

You must find excuses to laugh and to tell people in your life that you love them- on holidays, birthdays, and on ordinary days. But especially on ordinary days, for they can be the hardest of all.

And while you're busy loving everyone don't forget to also take time to nurture yourself. Treat yourself to long baths and light the expensive candles, wear lingerie alone, use the nice china, buy yourself flowers, cook yourself a nice meal, pleasure yourself, tell yourself you're beautiful when you look in the mirror, and start believing it. Dance when you feel like it, with music or without, with a warm body close to you or alone. Get lost searching the corners of your mind; watching the sunset; in conversations with yourself... and learn to cry, even if you don't know the reason for your tears.

Your heart is smarter than your head.

Trust it.

But above all, be fearless. The worst that could happen is death and that will come sooner or later anyways, whether you are ready or not (most people never are). So live, as if you were a young bird that just discovered flight. Don't just stay comfortable. Dive into the beautiful mess of life because death is right on the other side and we have all the time in the world for eternity.

So choose to live.

really live.

past your fears and others' ideas of what your life should be like.

It's ok to feel sad, negative feelings, but let them pass through you—don't get stuck in them. Let them go and come back to feeling your heart in its natural, beautiful state.

There's no need to panic over what's there. Relax into it and LET IT GO.

advice from a dream

they die

and you're reborn

you continue to live

and learn
with each breath

that life is what you make of it

and so is loss,

so is death.

every time you fall and get up

your legs get stronger

and so does

your heart.

we are never taught exactly how to walk away

there are no instructions for moving on

so every day goes on feeling same as the last

and only when we look back at the past

do we realize with how much strength

we were able to overcome heartache

give yourself some credit

because at the end of the day

you're surviving

when many others have given in

to despair.

when the healing comes

slowly at first, and then

all of a sudden

it will arrive without a timeline

and you will wonder why

salvation requires damnation

and grief demands

surrender.

You are not built on wishes but on the work

that you have invested into your heart and mind so

don't let them convince you there's a need to start fresh

just because 365 days have come to pass-

be who you are today.

You can't control the yesterdays of life or the promises of the future

but today is yours for the taking-

don't let it evaporate.

when the pain cuts deep

and you run out of tears and breath

and your heart feels as if it were only a sliver

of what it used to be

no one can be there to make it better,

to make you feel safe.

that's what my words are for.

that's why I write-

for my heart and yours and all the others

who have been shattered by life

and broken with loss

but who still hold on because they know that

hope is always the last

to die.

You don't need another half

just someone to match

the size of your heart and

strength of your love.

I woke up today having a case of the not enoughs: not fast enough, not fit enough, not strong enough, not lovable enough, not productive enough... even the good things in me I find aren't there enough, not holding their weight against the voice of my ego. I look deep into my eyes in the mirror and tell myself that I am beautiful, that my scars are badges of survival, the Purple Heart of the emotional wars I have fought in my life the last few years.

Starting over is hard. Growing is hard. Learning is hard. Letting go is hard. Loving yourself is hard. Opening up your heart is hard. And yet I've done all those things without him here. That is more enough than anything inside me could ever dare critique and tear apart.

Remember: you are much more than what you give yourself credit for.

When that little voice inside starts criticizing, tell it your story and remind it how much beauty lies in the strength that has carried you through.

some days are hard

life is hard

but you can't let it make you so.

stay soft. malleable. a dreamer.

that way when the difficulties come

you'll bend right over them

instead of just breaking in half

again.

what do they know
about living life without insurance
without a guarantee that things will
eventually fall together
instead of just falling apart
why can't they find the humor we see
in a savings account and
what a saving grace that indeed would be

but we don't get security
we get pray the pain away
keep the tears in
because we have to fight another day
They can't see it
but for us, life is a battle
there's a silent sadness we carry
between the lottery tickets and cash for a week's
worth of groceries we try to keep stashed
in our wallet of hope.

we protect ourselves so we don't shatter

but that keeps us from becoming whole

so then we stand there,

upright

with nowhere to go,

because breaking again isn't worth

taking the jump

and enjoying the fall.

the thing about sadness

is that you can't give it away.

It's yours to own.

But that doesn't mean you should keep it-

so let it come and let it go,

just like the currents

and don't forget

you're the whole goddamn ocean.

One day you wake up and you just find it there, as if it were sitting on a chair beside the bed, just waiting for you to wake up so it can say the words you had to live years to hear:

*You don't need to give so much of yourself to others
There's not ever enough you left for you.*

"There's not enough me left for me," you repeat to yourself. It is the wisest whisper you never knew you had been waiting for. Better even than the shiny ones he shared with you in bed that morning, when the blinds were shut past midday because even the sun couldn't pull you two apart. That chemistry was the culprit, the rascal that did you in, that made you cave and give too much of yourself away, much too soon again. And worst of all, without him deserving it.

Because you are the most precious gift.

Listen to that whisper.

Love yourself enough to keep plenty of you left for you.

sometimes you have to put your brain to sleep

for twelve hours straight so

your heart can continue

beating on

strong.

everyone wants a fresh start.

we just don't expect

having to go through

the pain of the end

in order to get

a new beginning.

it's ok to let go

to try and see

how far you can get

with eyes closed.

we keep breathing

we persevere
and rise above

half fearing and
half waiting
for our world to fall apart again

It's how we learn to live after the breaking-

the silver lining will never look the same.

tell your mind to be quiet and

give in to your heart

stop fighting the need inside you to pause.

breathe.

feel.

scream.

cry.

You are not a robot.

FEEL

feel deeply, painfully, without borders or end,

feel to infinity, and then,

feel again.

letting go is a process

and learning to let go

bittersweet

you get all the freedom

but no one to

share it with.

We keep track of how long it's been

since the day that shattered us

our brains do the math automatically

it's all so rational and surreal

time becomes a mere suggestion

a most realistic illusion

from the day we lose everything

and into the future.

the truth remains that there is always a silver lining

but it is also fair to wish

life didn't force us to search for it in the sky

every time it knocked us down

into the dirt.

there is much to gain from loss

if we just stop

constantly trying to prevent

another heartbreak.

surround yourself

with those who see your light

and wish still

to make it brighter.

how to survive darkness

broken pieces

can always be made whole again

no matter

how

they shattered.

I've been waking with the birds lately
so I can watch the sun rise and hear its truth clearly:
Each new day is a chance to start fresh.

You don't have to stay in the past.
That's done.
It's gone.
And life is wonderful if you
would just let it be, maybe even
learn to laugh a little bit.

Turns out the Universe has a sense of humor.

I know you would prefer silence over the words
you need to hear now:
No one else put up those walls or
locked the shackles tight around your heart
but you.

And you were right to do so–
We all have reasons and
excuses for our brokenness.

But we also hold the glue to
put ourselves together, we also have the
choice to move past the pain that shattered us.
We don't have to stay sad,
we don't have to build a home
out of darkness.

If you would just hope, trust, and let go
That's the secret, that's the key to the door
that holds your new beginning.
Then jump in, eyes closed,
mouth screaming like when you came out of your mother's womb
if you must
but don't let Spring pass you by just because you've grown
accustomed to the cold.

Go for the fresh start,
the new beginning,
go harvest the crop that sprouted
from all the seeds you planted with your tears,
go back to feeling like the person you once used to be.

Happy.

Free.

Maybe you barely even remember
the person you were before death,
the person you were before the pain of heartbreak,
the person you were before grief,
but I promise they're still there
just waiting for you to befriend them again.

If you would only listen.
If you would only let go

happiness

        will

            come.

it's a vicious cycle

we worry that we won't know

how to let go of all our

worries and concerns

when the time to let go

comes.

happiness

causes jealousy

because it requires

a lot of hard work

that very few people

want to do.

We try to convince ourselves that we have forever
to enjoy another sunset
and keep wishing for the days we had
when there's still so much ahead.

When the future comes knocking
open the door and let it in.

There's nothing left in the past
for you to keep now.

Let it go.

Trust that love will come again
just like it did then.

build a garden in your heart,

there, where the emptiness once sat,

feed it with light and love

and slowly you will find

life blooming

from the seed of your grief.

the best part of a broken heart

is the one that starts to heal

the one that refuses to stay torn apart

and slowly begins

to stitch itself

back up

the best part of a broken heart

is the one that

doesn't stay broken

for long.

In the process of losing him

I've gained a mom

found myself

fallen in love again

learned thick skin doesn't mean

everything they think it does

and stretched out my heart so big

the whole world can

fit in there

now.

Have I told you lately that I love you?

I love you because you stood up strong when the tempests of life came crashing down. I love that you use your words so bluntly, that you give your heart so entirely, and that you do it without ever expecting anything in return. I love that when a new day begins you decide to go when you could always stay. Stay in bed, stay the same, stay wild and untamed. And have you noticed that when you rub your eyes in the morning you never wipe off hope like so many do?

I love that about you.

don't waste life focusing on the losses

because if you're living fully

it's likely that you'll experience them quite often.

the secret is to hold on to the small things.

to the magic in your breath.

to any small gesture or experience that brings you bliss.

Hold on to the smiles and to the people

that put them on your face

and when the time comes

say thank you to grief

and let it go

in peace.

you're not more or less

of anything you've ever been

you're just finally growing into

the person you were always

meant to be.

trust your feet
when they begin walking towards a new horizon
trust your gut when it says *let go*

I promise your heart will soon catch up to your mind.
I promise soon tears of despair will be replaced with those of joy
I promise in time you will finally begin to realize
that you don't need to know
why everything happened.

You never did and
you never will.

It's time so say goodbye
to leave heartache behind,
my dear old friend.

and I have never been this ready
for a new beginning before,
I have never been this happy
about leaving the past behind
until now.

and maybe that's just the way life goes
some lose a lot on their way to get it all
lucky are we for surviving
for fighting through the tears
Fortunate are we
to have stood tall enough to see
that life is worth sticking around for.

How many have we lost
to the land of tears?
Far too many if you ask me.

And here we sit beneath the sun
expecting the clouds to roll in
just in case we have to run again at the first sign
of an incoming storm-

We have had to learn to be on the lookout,
we have had to learn to be on guard
strength comes accompanied by struggle
and by now we have become warriors
in our own fucking right.

making the bed

you tug and measure

and approximate calculations

to get the stretchy part of the sheet

to fit over the mattress

just right.

the rest is easy.

automatic, even.

the hardest part is always the start.

Death changes everything when it takes someone you love away.

You lose so much you start to live life waiting for your time to come too, afraid of ever caring deeply again. You know, *just in case*. Because now you feel in your bones the universal truth that **nothing** lasts forever. It's no longer just an idea floating around in your head. It's an ache, an open wound in the worst place, like on your fingertips. There is no rest from the fear of going through the worst again when you barely made it through before; when you're barely making it through now; when your head is still filled with endless regrets over the things you didn't do or say, as if your actions would have made a difference in the end.

You become irrational. And yet you are more rational that you have ever been.

Death does that.

And when you try to start to touch again, to feel again, it's right there- the ache throbbing, reminding you of the last time you felt that way and how it all disappeared in the end, like water that evaporates once it gets too hot. It is one of the most terrifying things a human can experience: to give up control of your heart while knowing that it will eventually end in loss and heartache.

Always.

Every. Single. time.

But that is the moment when you have to face your fears and let life and death figure it out between them. Because the funny thing about the aftermath of death is that only love can make you come alive again.

So when it knocks on your door, let love in.

You deserve a break from all the sadness death forgot to take back with him.

THE END

(or is it really the beginning?)